# Haunted Halloween

## 26 Chilling True Tales of Spooky October Nights and Paranormal Mysteries

By Lee Brickley

# Contents

# Introduction

Greetings, my esteemed reader, my name is Lee Brickley. Over the course of my life, I've dedicated myself to exploring the unseen, the ethereal, the enigmatic— those entities that lurk in the shadows and exist at the fringes of our understanding. I am a veteran paranormal investigator, having made countless journeys into the heart of the haunted, the eerie, and the otherworldly. My path has led me through the heavy silence of deserted graveyards, into the echoing emptiness of haunted houses, and deep into chilling mysteries that defy our conventional understanding of the world.

This journey of mine is not for those easily frightened or those unwilling to challenge their perception of the world around us. It's a journey into the deepest and darkest corners of our reality, where the laws that govern our world seemingly unravel, where the spectral and the uncanny hold sway. It's a journey that defies the ordinary, where the incredible is commonplace, and the unseen becomes seen.

In the pages of this book, 'Haunted Halloween: 26 Chilling True Tales of Spooky October Nights and Paranormal Mysteries,' I'm inviting you to embark with me on a journey into the extraordinary. Each tale is a recounting of one of my most chilling, unnerving, and thought-provoking cases, each one occurring on, or having a potent connection to, Halloween—the one night of the year when, as legend tells us, the veil between our world and the spirit world thins to near transparency.

The stories contained within this book span an array of settings, ranging from the quiet corners of suburban neighbourhoods, where normality prevails and paranormal activity seems an impossibility, to the very heart of eerie and legendary haunted sites, where history and the spectral intertwine. You'll read of spectral figures that appear amidst the frivolity of costume parades, of playful poltergeists causing mischief in pumpkin patches, of ghostly dancers waltzing through costume balls, and of strange, unexplainable occurrences in houses that should be abandoned but seem to be home to something beyond our comprehension.

Halloween is often viewed as a time of light-hearted fun and make-believe, a time when we don playful masks and become creatures of the night, when we gather sweets from our neighbours, and share stories designed to instil a playful fear. But as you'll discover in this collection of tales, sometimes those scary stories bear a kernel of truth. Sometimes, they are not merely stories woven to entertain around a bonfire; sometimes, they are chillingly, terrifyingly real.

Each of the tales in this collection, each investigation I undertook, has been exhaustively documented with the deepest respect for all those involved. The people whose lives were touched by these spectral phenomena, the locations that played host to these mysterious happenings, and even the spirits themselves—all have been considered and treated with the reverence they deserve. These are not the ghost stories you'll find in children's books or told around a campfire; they are true accounts of encounters with something beyond the realm of the understood, experiences that defy explanation and yet have been experienced by ordinary people, just like you and me.

My hope is that these stories not only thrill and chill, but that they also ignite a spark of curiosity within you. I hope that they offer a deeper understanding of the spectral world, and perhaps even provoke a healthy touch of fear about what might be silently observing from the shadows during those eerie Halloween nights. So, pull up a chair, dim the lights, wrap yourself in a blanket, and prepare a cup of your favourite hot beverage, for you are about to delve into the world of the unknown with me.

Welcome, dear reader, to 'Haunted Halloween.' I must ask you to leave your scepticism at the door, for what you are about to read will challenge what you believe to be possible. These aren't just tales spun to frighten and entertain... they are true accounts, personal experiences from the frontlines of the paranormal, from my lifelong journey into the spectral realm. I invite you now to turn the page, to embark on this journey with me, and to remember: these tales are a hauntingly real part of our world. Enjoy the journey, and as we say in our field—happy haunting.

# All Hallows Eve: The Ghost of the Victorian Mansion

Everyone loves a good ghost story on Halloween, don't they?" That's what was said to me when I first heard about the chilling experiences of the Henderson family. But let me assure you, this story is no campfire fable.

The Hendersons, a typical family of four, lived in an old Victorian mansion on the outskirts of London. The mansion had been a part of their family for generations, a great-aunt being the last relative to occupy it before them. After her passing, the Hendersons—David and Emily, along with their two children, Lily and Max—moved in, seeing it as an opportunity to escape the bustling city life for a quieter, more serene existence. They had no idea about the spectral tenant that already occupied their new home.

They moved into the house in early autumn, just in time to experience their first Halloween in the old mansion. The children were excited. What could be better than living in a real-life haunted house for Halloween? Little did they know how close their innocent excitement was to reality.

Halloween night arrived with an autumn chill in the air, and the crunch of fallen leaves underfoot. Emily had outdone herself decorating the mansion, adding a modern touch to the gothic architecture with spooky additions. Cobwebs were strung across the great arched door, orange and black streamers fluttered from the gargoyle-guarded eaves, and carved pumpkins stood like sentinels on the porch. The old house had never looked so alive, or so haunted.

The evening started like any other Halloween night. Max and Lily, dressed as a pirate and a fairy princess, respectively, went trick-or-treating around the town, their laughter echoing through the twilight. David and Emily handed out candies to the sporadic groups of trick-or-treaters brave enough to approach the imposing mansion. As the night deepened, the trick-or-treaters dwindled, leaving the Hendersons alone in their quiet, brooding mansion.

Emily was the first to notice the unusual happenings. As she was tidying up the leftover candies and decorations, she caught sight of a shadowy figure moving at the corner of her vision. She turned her head, but there was nothing there. A cold breeze swept through the room, causing her to shiver. She brushed it off as a draft, but the feeling of unease remained.

Meanwhile, David was upstairs, helping Max and Lily into their beds. Just as he was about to switch off the lights, he heard soft whispers, as though someone was talking in the next room. But the children were already drifting off to sleep, and Emily was downstairs. David felt a chill creeping up his spine. He attributed the sound to the age of the house. After all, old houses have a life of their own, don't they?

Later that night, as David and Emily settled down in their room, they noticed the temperature drop significantly.

Every creak of the house seemed amplified, echoing through the silent hallways. Emily commented on hearing the soft tinkling of piano keys, while David admitted to seeing shadows move from the corner of his eye. The couple laughed it off, attributing their fears to the spooky spirit of Halloween.

Their laughter died when they heard the sound of soft footsteps running down the hallway and the giggling of children. They rushed out, fearing Max and Lily might have woken up and were playing around. But they found them sound asleep in their rooms, oblivious to the eerie happenings.

As they climbed back into their bed, they noticed a framed family photo on the bedside table had been moved. Emily swore she had left it facing right, but now it was turned towards the left. The room felt colder, and the air had a heavy, electrifying presence.

Just past midnight, the real terror began. A loud thump echoed from the downstairs living room. Both David and

Emily jumped up. Racing down the stairs, they found a portrait of David's great-aunt lying face down. How it fell was a mystery as it was securely fastened to the wall.

David had barely set the portrait right when they heard the piano in the adjoining room playing a haunting melody. As they entered the room, the music stopped, but the piano keys were still vibrating from the recent contact. Nobody was there, yet the room felt crowded, the air heavy with the scent of roses, great-aunt's favourite perfume.

Terrified, they decided to gather the children and leave the house. But as they climbed the stairs, they saw her. A spectral figure, translucent and glowing, dressed in Victorian-era clothing, standing at the top of the staircase. It was the spitting image of David's great-aunt from the portraits. She looked at them, a sad smile on her face, and then vanished. That was their first encounter with the ghost.' The Victorian mansion wasn't just their inheritance —it was home to a piece of their family history that refused to leave.

This chilling experience marked the start of a series of events that turned their serene existence into a haunting ordeal, forever linking the Hendersons to the spectral world.

This is their Halloween tale—one of eerie melodies, spectral figures, and a connection to the other side. A story not of horror, but of inexplicable encounters and eternal family bonds. It reminds us that sometimes, the veil between the worlds can lift, and when it does, it changes lives forever.

# The Bewitching Hour: The Unseen Entity of Trick-or-Treat Street

Trick-or-Treat Street, as it was fondly called by the local children, was the heart of Halloween festivities in the suburban town of Somerset, Pennsylvania. Every house on the street would dress in their Halloween best, their yards a mix of playful and spooky decorations to enchant the trick-or-treaters. But behind the veil of cheer and chocolate bars, a chilling tale was woven into the very fabric of the street, a tale that unfolded every Halloween.

The whispers about Trick-or-Treat Street started innocently enough. Unsettling occurrences that were dismissed as figments of an overactive imagination or the result of too many ghost stories. Lights flickering, the sound of footsteps when no one was there, objects moving without any explanation, and a lingering sense of being watched. However, as years passed, the whispers grew louder, and the incidents became more frequent and more alarming.

Mysterious happenings took centre stage every All Hallows Eve, making the residents dread what was supposed to be a night of fun and frolic. The tales from Trick-or-Treat Street reached my ears through a local historian, an old friend with an uncanny knack for unearthing the unusual. The story was too intriguing, and the timing too perfect, to pass up the chance to investigate. I was on the next flight to Pennsylvania.

As I strolled down Trick-or-Treat Street on Halloween morning, I was greeted by smiling jack-o-lanterns, faux cobwebs adorning the fences, and inflatable ghouls swaying in the breeze. But beneath the festive veneer, an unsettling silence hung in the air. The houses, despite their cheerful exterior, seemed to carry an eerie secret.

The Williams' house was my first stop, their story being the most chilling of all. A hard working couple with two teenage children, the Williams were the embodiment of the American dream. But come Halloween, they found themselves at the epicentre of the unexplainable.

One particular Halloween, their youngest, Sam, was home alone while the rest of the family were out trick-or-treating. He claimed to have heard a knock at the door, and expecting late trick-or-treaters, he opened it. However, instead of a group of costumed kids, he found no one there. The street was empty, the only sound was the rustling of dry leaves on the pavement.

Thinking it to be a prank, Sam closed the door. But as he turned, he saw the shadow of a tall figure in the hallway. Before he could react, the figure disappeared. In its place was a small, antique silver pendant, lying innocuously on the floor. No one in the family recognized it, and where it came from is still a mystery.

At the Petersons' next door, their story was eerily similar.

Mrs. Peterson spoke of a Halloween night when she found her kitchen in complete disarray. The refrigerator door was wide open, every drawer and cabinet was ajar, and her pots and pans were scattered all over the floor. There was no sign of a break-in, and the rest of the house was untouched. Even more chilling, she confessed to having seen fleeting shadows in her peripheral vision.

As I went from one house to another, everyone had a tale to tell. Some heard whispering voices in the dead of night, others reported their belongings inexplicably moving around, and a few even claimed to have seen apparitions. All incidents occurred on Halloween, and every family had one common experience - the feeling of an unseen presence.

I spent Halloween night on Trick-or-Treat Street, waiting for the mysterious entity to make its presence known. As the street buzzed with children in costumes and the air filled with laughter and the rustle of candy wrappers, I felt a shift in the atmosphere. The air turned colder, and a sense of unease crept up on me.

Just as the clock struck midnight, the lights in every house on the street flickered simultaneously. A cold breeze swept the street, and a shadow, tall and looming, seemed to move swiftly down the row of houses. And then, as quickly as it had started, it was over. The lights stopped flickering, the wind died down, and the shadow was gone. All that was left was the echo of an eerie silence.

Whether it was a shared hallucination, a trick of the light, or something beyond our understanding, the residents of Trick-or-Treat Street were united in their belief of the unseen entity. They were living in their own real-life ghost story, a chilling saga that unfolded every Halloween night. The unseen entity of Trick-or-Treat Street serves as a chilling reminder of the thin veil between our world and the unknown during the witching hour of All Hallows Eve.

# Cursed Candy: The Spectral Presence in the Candy Factory

There's a certain magic that lives in the heart of a candy factory, a joy and delight that tickles the child in us all. But in the town of Portville, New York, an old candy factory held more than just confectionary delights. It held a chilling secret that came to light every Halloween.

The Portville Candy Factory had been a part of the town's landscape for over a century. It was known far and wide for its delicious treats and for a ghost story that had been passed down through the generations. The story told of a factory worker, a man named Jacob Ellis, who tragically lost his life in an accident involving a candy mixer in the late

1800s.

Jacob was known to be a diligent worker, often staying late to perfect his candy recipes. On that fateful Halloween night, Jacob had been alone in the factory. The details of his accident remain murky, but the end result was a hauntingly tragic loss.

After Jacob's death, strange things began happening at the candy factory. The first incident happened the following Halloween. Workers reported hearing strange noises, like a rhythmic tapping echoing through the otherwise silent factory. It was soft at first, easy to dismiss as the usual noises of an old building, but as the night grew darker, the tapping grew louder and turned into a horrifying clatter, as if someone was operating the machines.

As the years passed, the phenomena became more alarming. Lights flickered, machinery turned on and off without explanation, and items moved from their place. Workers reported an uncanny sensation of being watched, and the faint smell of caramel, Jacob's favourite candy, would sometimes fill the factory.

Despite the eerie occurrences, the factory continued to operate. The incidents, confined to Halloween night, became an accepted part of the factory's lore, a chilling tale shared with new employees and visitors. The factory workers came to believe that Jacob's spirit had never left the factory, his love for his craft binding him to this world.

When I arrived in Portville, the factory had been closed for several years. A decline in demand and the unsettling rumours about the factory's spectral inhabitant had forced its doors shut. The once lively hub of sweet delights was now a quiet, brooding structure, its darkened windows reflecting the town's fears.

I was given access to the factory on Halloween night, the night when Jacob was known to make his presence felt. As I stepped into the deserted factory, a shiver ran down my spine. The air was stale, and a layer of dust had settled over the machinery. It was a picture of abandonment, a stark contrast to the hustle and bustle that once filled the space.

As I walked through the factory, I could almost hear the echo of laughter, the clatter of candy-making machines, and the sweet aroma of confections. The silence was thick, hanging heavily around me. With every tick of the clock, I felt an increase in the air's density, a growing pressure that had me on edge.

Midnight was when the activity was reported to peak. With my equipment set up, I waited. Just as the clock struck twelve, a cold breeze swept through the factory. The stillness was broken by a soft humming, reminiscent of the factory machinery. The scent of caramel filled the air, growing stronger with each passing second. The lights started to flicker, and a shadowy figure appeared, flitting between the machines.

The shadowy figure was tall and thin, bearing a striking resemblance to the photographs I had seen of Jacob. It moved with purpose, pausing by the old candy mixer where Jacob had met his untimely end. And then, as quickly as it had appeared, it was gone. The scent of caramel lingered in the air, a sweet reminder of the spectral presence I had just encountered.

The spectral presence in the candy factory served as a poignant reminder of a life cut short and a love for a craft that transcended the boundaries of life and death. It was a Halloween tale not of horror, but of tragedy and eternal dedication. And for me, it was yet another example of the inexplicable mysteries that our world holds, the mysteries that make every Halloween a journey into the unknown.

# Spirits of the Harvest Moon: Paranormal Phenomena in the Pumpkin Patch

In the picturesque farming town of West Haven, Vermont, lay the sprawling Sullivan Farm, renowned for its vast pumpkin patch. Come autumn, the farm would transform into a golden haven of ripe pumpkins, drawing visitors from all around to pick their own pumpkins for Halloween. But the Sullivan Pumpkin Patch held a secret as old as the farm itself.

For generations, the Sullivans had whispered tales of ghostly apparitions and strange occurrences that took place in the pumpkin patch every Halloween. The story was always the same - as the Harvest Moon rose on All Hallows

Eve, the pumpkin patch would become a hotbed of paranormal activity. Lights would be seen darting between the rows of pumpkins, strange shadows would flit about, and an eerie silence would fall upon the farm, a silence so profound it felt as if time itself had stopped.

My interest piqued by the tale, I found myself heading to Vermont in the days leading up to Halloween. Greeted by the charming Sullivans and their sea of pumpkins, I could feel an underlying energy, a sort of anticipation that hung in the cool autumn air. This energy, the family matriarch told me, was a signal of the spectral gathering to come.

The Sullivans were descendants of Irish settlers who had been among the first to farm in West Haven. They had brought with them the Samhain traditions, marking the end of the harvest season and the start of winter, a time when the veil between the living and the dead was believed to be its thinnest. This tradition had seamlessly blended into the Halloween celebrations, but for the Sullivans, it remained a night of reverence for the spirits.

As I was led through the pumpkin patch, I could see the love and hard work that went into the farm. The pumpkins, large and ripe, were a sight to behold under the autumn sun. But as dusk fell, the cheerful orange field took on an eerie quality. The scarecrows seemed to watch us with unseen eyes, and the rustling leaves sounded like whispered secrets.

I was offered a seat on the farmhouse porch, from where I had a clear view of the pumpkin patch. As the moon rose, casting long shadows between the pumpkins, I felt a shift in the atmosphere. It was subtle, a slight drop in temperature, a soft rustle passing through the pumpkin leaves. And then, just as the clock struck midnight, it began.

Lights appeared within the pumpkin patch, like hundreds of fireflies, casting an ethereal glow on the ripened pumpkins. The lights danced around, weaving through the patch in a seemingly choreographed spectacle. Then, shadows began to flit around the edges of the field, human-like but without form. They moved around the patch, sometimes pausing by a particular pumpkin, sometimes seemingly interacting with the lights.

The sight was mesmerising and uncanny. It wasn't terrifying in the traditional sense, but it made the hairs at the back of my neck stand up, a testament to the otherworldly event unfolding before my eyes. It went on for what felt like hours, this ethereal ballet, until the first light of dawn started to creep into the sky. As the sun rose, the lights gradually faded, and the shadows dissipated, leaving behind a calm and serene pumpkin patch.

The Sullivans believe these apparitions and phenomena are the spirits of their ancestors, visiting their old home on the one night they can. To them, Halloween isn't just about costumes and candy, it's a night when they feel a deep connection with their roots, their history. And having witnessed it, I can attest that the experience is profoundly moving, a magical spectacle that blurs the boundaries between the physical and the spiritual world.

The Spirits of the Harvest Moon in the Sullivan Pumpkin Patch are a testament to the mysterious charm of

Halloween. It's a phenomenon that challenges our understanding of the world, pushing us to look beyond the surface and delve into the unknown. This Halloween tale serves as a poignant reminder that sometimes, the things that scare us can also be the things that connect us to our past and our heritage.

# Jack-O'-Lantern Jinx: The Haunting at the Carving Contest

Every town has its traditions, and for the residents of Fall Creek, Oregon, it was the annual pumpkin carving contest held on Halloween. It was a charming and festive event, the highlight of the town's fall celebrations, a chance for neighbours to showcase their creativity and craftsmanship. However, in recent years, this beloved tradition had been marred by a series of unexplained events.

Unusual incidents began occurring at the contest about a decade ago. Perfectly carved pumpkins would be mysteriously smashed, unseen forces seemed to trip contestants, and tools would disappear only to reappear in odd places. The townsfolk began to suspect that they were not alone in their festivities.

At first, the residents dismissed these incidents as pranks, attributing them to over-excited children or mischievous teenagers. But as the disturbances persisted year after year, growing more unpredictable and unsettling, whispers of a haunting started to circulate.

Intrigued by the tale of the Jack-O'-Lantern Jinx, as it had come to be known, I made my way to Fall Creek. Nestled amidst a canopy of autumn hues, the small town was a perfect postcard of Halloween spirit. The anticipation for the upcoming pumpkin carving contest was palpable.

On the eve of Halloween, I met with the contest organisers, a group of dedicated and enthusiastic locals. They shared their experiences of the strange occurrences, a mix of unease and excitement in their voices. They hoped that the contest would proceed without disruption this year, but a part of them seemed resigned to the expected chaos.

As Halloween dawned, the town square came alive with the hustle and bustle of the carving contest. The air was crisp, filled with the sweet smell of ripe pumpkins and the infectious laughter of the excited participants. Carving stations were set up, each contestant eagerly awaiting the start of the contest.

And then, right on cue, as the contest began, so did the disturbances. It started subtly - a soft gust of wind sending a pile of carving tools clattering to the ground, a contestant yelping as their pumpkin inexplicably rolled off their table. But as the day progressed, the incidents became increasingly disruptive.

Pumpkins that had been carefully carved were found ruined, their intricate designs morphed into grotesque faces. A sudden chill seemed to descend over the square, causing shivers to run down spines. Laughter turned into whispers of worry, and the jovial atmosphere gave way to an uneasy anticipation of the next disruption.

The climax of the jinx's antics occurred just as the contest was drawing to a close. Suddenly, all the jack-o'-lanterns flickered to life, their eerie glows bathing the square in an unsettling light. This spectacle lasted for a few minutes before they abruptly extinguished, plunging the area into darkness. A cold wind swept across the square, causing gasps of surprise and alarm among the gathered crowd.

When the lights came back on, a collective gasp echoed through the square. All the ruined pumpkins had been restored to their original, carefully carved designs, even more vibrant and intricate than before. The contest ended on this bewildering note, with the participants and spectators alike in awe of the turn of events.

The Haunting at the Carving Contest had been a truly unusual encounter. It wasn't frightening or menacing, but it was undoubtedly paranormal. The spirit of the jinx seemed to be a mischievous one, causing chaos and confusion but ultimately adding to the unique charm of the town's Halloween celebrations.

This Halloween tale serves as a reminder of the unexpected

forms in which the paranormal can manifest. Not all ghost stories are meant to terrify; some, like the Jack-O'-Lantern Jinx, bring with them an element of playfulness and mystery, making Halloween a truly enchanting time.

# Masked Apparition: The Haunting of the Halloween Store

The Costume Castle, a thriving Halloween store in Salem, Massachusetts, had been a one-stop destination for Halloween supplies for over two decades. Every year, from early September until Halloween, locals and tourists would throng the store, hunting for the perfect costume, props, and decorations.

However, strange things had been happening in the store for the past few years, all revolving around an ornate, vintage mask. The mask, an elegant piece adorned with feathers and gemstones, was a remnant from the store's early days, and despite its beauty, no one ever purchased it.

Customers and employees alike reported feeling an uncanny chill whenever they were near it, and some even claimed to have seen a shadowy figure wearing the mask after hours.

As a paranormal investigator, the tale of the Masked Apparition garnered my interest. A haunting centred around a particular object was not unheard of, and the fact that this was happening in a Halloween store, in a town renowned for its witch trials, made it even more compelling.

Upon arriving at the Costume Castle, I was immediately taken by its vibrant atmosphere. The store was a Halloween lover's paradise, filled with an array of costumes, props, and decorations. But amidst the joviality, the vintage mask hung on the wall, casting an ominous shadow.

The store's employees were eager to share their experiences with the haunted mask. They spoke of unexplained cold spots around the mask, of hearing whispers late at night, and of seeing a spectral figure wandering the store after hours, always near the mask. Customers, too, recounted similar experiences, some even vowing never to return to the store after a particularly chilling encounter.

I decided to stay at the store overnight, hoping to witness the Masked Apparition. As the last customers left and the employees locked up for the night, a sense of unease began to settle in. The store, once filled with the sounds of laughter and excitement, was eerily silent, the quiet only broken by the occasional creak of a display stand.

As I settled down near the mask, I couldn't shake off the sensation of being watched. It felt as though the eyes behind the mask were alive, observing my every move. The temperature around the mask was noticeably colder, a common sign of a paranormal presence.

Just as the clock struck midnight, a gust of wind swept through the store. The lights flickered before plunging the store into darkness. I felt a presence, strong and overwhelming, moving around the room. I turned on my flashlight, and my heart skipped a beat. There, standing across the room, was the apparition.

It was a tall figure, shrouded in darkness, but unmistakably wearing the vintage mask. The mask seemed to come alive on the figure, the gemstones sparkling in the torchlight. The figure moved around the store, seeming to glide over the floor, never straying too far from the mask's original place.

I watched in awe as the spectral figure moved around. It seemed peaceful, almost melancholy, trapped in its own world. As the sun began to rise, the figure faded away, leaving behind the vintage mask, now lying on the floor.

The Haunting of the Halloween Store was unlike any I had encountered before. It was a haunting borne out of attachment, a spirit seemingly tethered to a mask, a remnant from a different time. The mask wasn't just a Halloween prop; it was a link to the past, to a story untold, to a spirit that found solace in the familiar.

Halloween, for all its fun and revelry, can also be a time of reflection and remembrance, a time when the past can bleed into the present, creating experiences that defy explanation. The Masked Apparition served as a poignant reminder of this, adding another chilling tale to the lore of Halloween.

# Costume Parade Phantom: The Ghost of Main Street

Every year on Halloween, the otherwise quiet town of St. Augustine, Florida, is filled with revelry as they host their annual costume parade. The locals and tourists, donned in costumes ranging from the whimsical to the terrifying, take to Main Street to celebrate the spookiest night of the year. But this festive event has, over the years, become infamous for a more eerie reason - the repeated sightings of a spectral figure that marches alone at the end of the parade.

The first sighting of the Costume Parade Phantom, as the figure was now known, was reported a little over two decades ago. According to spectators, once the parade was over and the last of the costumed revellers had passed by, a lone figure could be seen marching down the deserted street. Dressed in a Civil War-era uniform, the figure seemed out of place and time. Those who saw him reported feeling an intense cold and a profound sense of sorrow.

When I first heard about the Costume Parade Phantom, I was intrigued. A spectral soldier marching down a modern parade seemed out of a Gothic novel. The fact that the sightings happened only during the Halloween parade added to the mystery. I knew I had to investigate.

Upon reaching St. Augustine, I was immediately swept up in the Halloween spirit. The town was abuzz with excitement for the upcoming parade. As I spoke with the locals, I realised that the Phantom had become a part of their Halloween tradition. Some viewed him with fear, while others saw him as a spectral guardian of the parade.

Halloween arrived with much fanfare. The costume parade was a sight to behold, with everyone putting their best foot forward. As the parade neared its end, I positioned myself towards the end of the route, the location where the Phantom had been sighted most often.

As the last of the costumed participants passed, a palpable shift occurred. The air turned colder, and a hush fell over the crowd. And then, out of the shadows, he emerged - the Costume Parade Phantom.

The spectral figure was tall and imposing, dressed in a Civil War uniform. His presence was as tangible as the chill in the air. He marched with a determination that seemed at odds with the eeriness of the situation. The crowd watched in silent awe as the phantom soldier marched down Main Street before fading away.

The experience left me with a mix of feelings - awe, wonder, and a touch of melancholy. The Phantom wasn't a terrifying presence; rather, he was a reminder of a past that the town had forgotten. His appearance at the costume parade, a celebration of the fantastical and the make-believe, seemed fitting. It was as if the Phantom used the revelry as a cover to step out from the annals of history, to remind the town of its past.

The Ghost of Main Street is a poignant tale of a spectral

soldier who has become a part of the town's Halloween tradition. His presence serves as a reminder that the past and the present often collide on Halloween, blurring the lines between the living and the dead, the real and the imagined. This tale is a testament to the magic and mystery of Halloween, a night when the ordinary can turn extraordinary, and when a costume parade can become a march through history.

# Broomstick Shadows: The Witch of the Willow Woods

The dense, ominous Willow Woods, nestled in the outskirts of the quaint town of Glastonbury, Vermont, had always been shrouded in mystery and folklore. Over the years, it has earned a reputation for being haunted, with hikers and residents repeatedly reporting sightings of a spectral witch-like figure floating among the trees, appearing exclusively on All Hallows' Eve.

According to local lore, the forest was once the dwelling place of a solitary woman named Agnes, known for her knowledge of herbal remedies. In a town struck by superstition, Agnes's unorthodox lifestyle led to her being labelled a witch. However, there were no historical records or concrete evidence to verify these stories, making Agnes a figure of legend and speculation.

When I heard the intriguing tale of the Witch of the Willow Woods, I felt a powerful pull to uncover the truth. Was Agnes real, or was she merely a product of town folklore? And if she was real, did her spirit linger in the forest, making appearances each Halloween? I resolved to spend Halloween night in the forest, bracing myself for whatever mysteries the Willow Woods chose to reveal.

As I ventured into the woods on the eve of Halloween, the ambiance took an eerie turn. The forest seemed to come alive, whispering untold secrets through the rustling leaves and creaking branches. As night fell, the forest was bathed in an ethereal moonlight, casting long, haunting shadows that danced upon the forest floor. Every snap of a twig or rustle of leaves set my heart racing, adding to the growing sense of anticipation.

Sitting amidst the towering trees, I felt an odd sense of serenity mixed with a creeping trepidation. I could feel the energy shift around me as midnight approached. A sudden chill swept through the forest, and I could see my breath fogging up in the cold air, despite it being an unusually warm autumn night.

As the church bell in the distant town struck midnight, a sudden burst of wind rattled the forest canopy. An eerie light began to radiate from deeper within the woods. Bracing myself, I ventured towards it. As I made my way through the dense foliage, I saw her. There, hovering above the forest floor, was the spectral figure of a woman.

Dressed in a ragged cloak, she floated gracefully amongst the trees. Her ghostly figure was barely visible, but the moonlight gave her an otherworldly glow. She seemed to be riding a broomstick, true to the witch folklore, but her presence was far from menacing. She moved in harmony with the forest, a part of it rather than an intruder.

I watched as the spectral figure drifted amongst the trees, lost in a world of her own. As the witch-like figure faded with the first light of dawn, I was left with a sense of awe and a newfound understanding.

The Witch of the Willow Woods was not a symbol of fear but a beacon of the misunderstood. Whether she was the spirit of Agnes or a manifestation of the town's collective folklore, she served as a reminder that sometimes, fear and superstition can cast shadows far scarier than the entities they purport to represent.

The tale of the Broomstick Shadows adds a layer of depth to our Halloween lore. It serves as a reminder that beneath the costumes and candy, Halloween is a time when the veil between the physical and spiritual world thins, allowing us a glimpse into the unknown, into tales of misunderstood beings, and into the realms of the extraordinary. And it's these moments, these glimpses, that make Halloween the uniquely chilling and fascinating celebration it is.

# Graveyard Whispers: The Tale of the Halloween Séance

The sleepy town of Binghamton, New York, holds a dark secret. Its oldest graveyard, a sprawling expanse of weathered tombstones and moss-covered crypts, is home to a tale of paranormal activity that would make even the most hardened sceptic's blood run cold. This tale involves a group of friends, a séance on a Halloween night, and a series of events that turned their curious dabbling into a harrowing encounter with the unseen.

The story begins with five friends: Anna, Charlie, Beth, David, and Emily. Known for their adventurous spirit and fascination with the supernatural, they decided to conduct a séance on Halloween night. They believed that the thin veil between the living and the dead during this period would yield an unforgettable experience. Little did they know, they were indeed stepping into an unforgettable night, albeit one marked by terror and mystery.

The decision to hold the séance in the graveyard added an extra layer of eeriness to their plan. As an investigator of the paranormal, I found their experience intriguing, and so, decided to delve into the story of the Halloween Séance.

On Halloween night, under a cloudless sky, they assembled in the graveyard. The silhouettes of the tombstones stood like silent sentinels, veiled in the gloom. The only light came from the pale glow of the moon and the flickering candles they had arranged in a circle for their séance. As they began their ritual, an uneasy calm descended on the graveyard.

They called out to the spirits, their voices echoing eerily amongst the tombstones. Minutes turned into hours, but there was no response. Just as they were about to call it a night, a chilling breeze swept across the graveyard, extinguishing the candles. The sudden plunge into darkness was followed by a disconcerting whisper that seemed to come from nowhere and everywhere at once.

Overwhelmed by fear, they scrambled to light their candles. By the flickering light, they saw a shadowy figure standing at the edge of their circle. It stood there for a moment, an oppressive figure cloaked in the darkness, before vanishing as abruptly as it had appeared.

Panic ensued. The friends hastily ended their séance and fled from the graveyard, leaving behind a circle of half-extinguished candles and an air of unspeakable dread. The experience left them shaken, forever changing their perspective on the spirit world.

Recounting the tale of the Halloween séance, I couldn't help but feel a shiver down my spine. The graveyard, the séance, and the unexpected response they received, combined to form a hauntingly spooky tale, the echoes of which still linger in the silent corners of the graveyard.

The tale of the Graveyard Whispers serves as a stark reminder that Halloween is more than just costumes and candy. It's a night when the boundary between our world and the next blurs, when the ordinary can give way to the extraordinary, and when a seemingly harmless séance can turn into a chilling encounter.

It also underlines a profound respect for the unknown that often escapes us in our quest for understanding. After all, some doors, once opened, reveal more than we're prepared to confront. This Halloween tale, filled with mystery and intrigue, is one such door, reminding us that the whispers we seek might just answer back.

# Black Cat Crossing: The Cursed Street of the Suburbs

In the serene suburb of Ashford Heights, a picturesque neighbourhood known for its cherry blossom-lined streets and picket-fenced houses, there exists a strange anomaly. Here, the otherwise familiar and reassuringly mundane scene is punctuated by a streak of the extraordinary. Every Halloween, a peculiar phenomenon occurs that has left the residents of Elm Street both intrigued and perturbed.

According to local residents, each Halloween, a black cat makes its appearance on Elm Street. The cat, with its shining emerald-green eyes and sleek black fur, isn't merely a neighbourhood pet straying too far from home. No, this black cat carries an aura of mystery that sends chills down the spine of even the bravest souls.

The cat seems to bring in its wake an assortment of strange happenings. Electronics fail, objects move without any apparent cause, shadows dance in the corner of the eye, and an eerie sensation of being watched pervades the entire street. It's as though the cat's presence stirs up the latent paranormal energy of Elm Street, causing the usually quiet suburb to transform into a hotbed of spectral activity.

As a paranormal investigator, the tale of the Black Cat Crossing piqued my curiosity. I decided to spend Halloween night on Elm Street, hoping to encounter the mysterious cat and witness the strange phenomena it supposedly induced.

On Halloween night, Elm Street was a picture of suburban celebration. Children, dressed in costumes, scampered from house to house, collecting candy. Decorated pumpkins adorned the porches, and the air was filled with laughter and cheer. It was hard to believe that this cheerful scene could transform into something otherworldly.

As the evening wore on, the laughter faded, and the children retreated, leaving behind a haunting quietness. As the clock struck midnight, there was a shift in the air. The lights in the houses along the street began to flicker inexplicably. Then, like a whisper of the night itself, the black cat appeared.

Its green eyes glowed in the moonlight as it sauntered down the street, a spectral figure against the backdrop of silent houses. A shiver ran down my spine as I observed the cat, feeling an inexplicable sense of unease.

As the cat moved further down the street, strange things began to occur. A child's swing in one of the gardens started to sway ominously on its own. Windows rattled, and the eerie figure of a man could be seen in the reflection, despite there being no one around. Shadows flickered and danced in ways that made the hair on the back of my neck stand on end. The laughter and cheer of earlier in the evening seemed like a distant memory, replaced by an eerie stillness.

As dawn approached, the cat disappeared as subtly as it had appeared, and the peculiar occurrences ceased. Elm Street returned to its usual calm, leaving behind only whispers of the night's eerie happenings.

The tale of the Black Cat Crossing serves as a chilling reminder of the unknown that lurks in the shadows of our everyday lives. This Halloween story, nestled in the heart of a picturesque suburb, underscores the intriguing mystery that a single night can hold. It teaches us that even in the most familiar of places, the extraordinary can make its presence felt, blurring the boundaries between the ordinary and the paranormal, the explained and the unexplained, the living, and the dead. It's a tale that will forever be remembered in the hushed whispers of Elm Street, a tale that brings an eerie excitement to each approaching Halloween.

# The October Poltergeist: The Mystery of the Abandoned House

On the outskirts of the small town of Wimberley, Texas, a dilapidated house lay shrouded in mystery and a palpable sense of foreboding. The house, once a proud symbol of Victorian architecture, now stood deserted, its grandeur replaced by decay. Its empty windows gazed blankly at the passing of time, and its once-lush garden was now overrun by weeds. The townsfolk avoided the old house, referring to it simply as "the abandoned house." Their avoidance, however, was not due merely to its state of disrepair but was fueled by fear.

A local legend had it that every October, the house would

come alive with inexplicable poltergeist activity. Inanimate objects would move of their own accord, doors would slam shut, windows would shatter, and an eerie presence could be felt. The intensity of this activity was said to increase as Halloween approached, reaching a terrifying crescendo on the night itself.

The story of the October Poltergeist intrigued me as a paranormal investigator. I decided to spend the days leading up to Halloween at the house, hoping to experience and document the alleged paranormal phenomena.

I arrived in Wimberley a week before Halloween. The first glimpse of the abandoned house sent an involuntary shiver down my spine. Its weathered façade bore an expression of desolation, its vacant windows gaping like hollow eyes. I could feel a distinct energy emanating from the house, a silent hum that pervaded its air of neglect.

Over the next few days, I set up my equipment and began my vigil. At first, the house remained silent, its mysteries locked away. As October days passed, however, I started witnessing unusual events. Objects would inexplicably move from their original place, and chilling breezes would gust through closed windows. The house seemed to come alive in the oddest ways.

As Halloween approached, the poltergeist activity intensified. One night, I awoke to the sound of shattering glass. I rushed downstairs to find the living room in disarray, with furniture overturned and windows broken. There was a heaviness in the air, a palpable sense of unease that seemed to grow with each passing minute.

On Halloween night, the atmosphere in the house was electric. As the clock struck midnight, a cacophony erupted. Doors slammed, items flew across rooms, and the walls echoed with an eerie whisper. Despite the terror I felt, I couldn't help but marvel at the raw power of the phenomena occurring around me.

As the first rays of dawn broke, the house returned to its former state of unsettling silence. It was as if the storm of paranormal activity had never occurred, leaving behind only the wreckage as evidence of the previous night's events.

The mystery of the October Poltergeist was a terrifying exploration into the realm of the unknown. It underscored the thin line that separates our reality from the otherworldly, reminding us that, sometimes, that line can blur.

As a tale of Halloween, it carries an extra layer of spookiness, playing into our deepest fears and fascination with the unseen. It is a tale that will linger long after the lights have been turned off, a tale that adds an extra chill to the autumnal October air. This haunted house, with its October Poltergeist, has been etched into the annals of the paranormal world, standing as a chilling testament to the mysteries that sometimes lie hidden within the walls of the ordinary.

# Apparitions in the Apple Orchard: The Spirits of the Harvest

Nestled in the heart of the Hudson Valley, the Jacobs family had been tending to their sprawling apple orchard for generations. The orchard, a picturesque tapestry of golden leaves and plump, red apples, was an integral part of their family tradition, particularly during the harvest season. Each year, as October rolled around, the Jacobs would come together to pick apples, a wholesome ritual that was treasured by all. However, this quaint family tradition took an eerie turn when the family started experiencing spectral apparitions in their orchard every Halloween.

As the stories of the haunted apple orchard reached my

ears, I was intrigued. The idea of a place so intrinsically tied to familial warmth and tradition harbouring spectral entities was paradoxically chilling. I decided to delve into this uncanny occurrence and arrived at the Jacobs' estate a week before Halloween.

The orchard was a vision of autumnal beauty, its rows of apple trees standing tall against the clear October sky. Despite its serene appearance, I could sense an undercurrent of unease in the air, a sense of anticipation that made the hairs on the back of my neck stand on end.

My first encounter with the spectral apparitions occurred on a crisp, moonlit night. I was walking through the orchard when a sudden chill swept over me. The temperature around me dropped drastically, and I could see my breath fogging up in the cool air. As I turned around, I saw a figure emerging from the rows of apple trees. The figure was translucent, its form flickering like an old television set struggling to maintain a signal.

The apparition glided through the orchard, seemingly

unaware of my presence. It moved with an otherworldly grace, passing through the apple trees, leaving a trail of frost in its wake. The sight was eerily beautiful yet profoundly unsettling.

As Halloween approached, the spectral activity in the apple orchard increased. Multiple apparitions appeared each night, drifting aimlessly among the trees. Some apparitions seemed to be reenacting mundane tasks, like picking apples or tending to the trees. It was as if they were reliving snippets of their lives, stuck in a perpetual loop of their own making.

The climax of these spectral occurrences happened on Halloween night. The orchard was abuzz with an ethereal energy. Apparitions materialised all around, their ghostly forms illuminated by the glow of the harvest moon. A spectral procession unfolded before my eyes, the phantoms moving in a solemn march through the orchard. The air was filled with an inexplicable sense of melancholy, a silent narrative of lives once lived.

As the sun rose on the morning of November 1st, the spectral parade faded away, leaving behind an eerily silent apple orchard. The veil that had lifted for the spirits to cross over had once again descended, marking an end to the ghostly performances of the harvest season.

The tale of the Apparitions in the Apple Orchard is a chilling testament to the mysteries that shroud the world beyond our understanding. It speaks of a thin veil separating the living from the dead, a veil that occasionally lifts to reveal a world that exists parallel to ours. This haunting Halloween tale is a reminder of the uncanny occurrences that sometimes seep into our ordinary lives, transforming familiar traditions into eerie experiences that linger long after the jack-o'-lanterns have been extinguished.

# Tales from the Corn Maze:

# The Lost Souls of Halloween

In the small town of Ravenswood, New Hampshire, the annual Halloween corn maze was an event cherished by locals and tourists alike. Designed in a different pattern each year and sprawling across multiple acres, the corn maze was a true marvel of autumn. However, behind its playful façade, the maze held a darker secret, known only to a few who dared venture into its labyrinthine paths after sunset. It was whispered that visitors would often find themselves lost in more than just the twists and turns of the maze.

As a paranormal investigator, I have always been intrigued by such tales. They held the promise of an unknown world veiled by the apparent normalcy of everyday life. So, when I first heard about the uncanny incidents linked to the Ravenswood Corn Maze, I was drawn to explore its mysteries.

I arrived in Ravenswood on the eve of Halloween. The town was buzzing with the excitement of the upcoming festivities, the corn maze being the crown jewel of these celebrations. The maze was nestled at the edge of town, the tall corn stalks casting long shadows in the afternoon sun. There was a disconcerting quietness around it that stood in stark contrast to the jubilant atmosphere in town.

As the day turned into night, I prepared to venture into the maze. Armed with a flashlight and a sense of growing anticipation, I took the first step into the labyrinth. The corn stalks towered over me, their rustling in the cool breeze creating an eerie symphony of whispers.

For the first hour, it felt like a regular maze – challenging, intriguing, and fun. But as the night deepened, the atmosphere began to change.

The whispers of the corn grew louder, and I felt an unshakeable feeling of being watched. The path ahead grew increasingly unfamiliar, even though I was sure I had crossed it before. It was as if the maze was reshaping itself, the corn stalks shifting around me in a sinister dance.

Then, I saw it. An apparition. It emerged from the corn stalks, its form hazy and flickering like a candle in the wind. I froze in place as the ghostly figure walked past me, oblivious to my presence. The air turned colder, and I could hear a distant echo of sorrowful whispers. The figure vanished as suddenly as it had appeared, leaving me alone in the chilling silence of the maze.

The rest of the night was a series of spectral encounters. Ghostly figures appeared and disappeared, each seemingly trapped in their own slice of time. Some seemed aware of their surroundings, while others were entirely engrossed in their own spectral existence. Each encounter was as eerie as the last, the apparitions adding a supernatural layer to the disorientation of the maze.

As the first rays of dawn touched the sky, I finally emerged from the maze. The ghostly inhabitants had vanished, and the corn maze returned to its ordinary state, its supernatural aura fading away with the darkness.

The Tale from the Corn Maze was a hair-raising journey into the unknown. It was a stark reminder that sometimes, the most innocuous places can be a portal to the supernatural. The maze wasn't just a fun Halloween attraction; it was a purgatory where lost souls roamed, making their presence known to those who dared venture into their domain on All Hallows' Eve. A thrilling exploration of the unseen world, this tale is a haunting testament to the mysteries of the paranormal that exist in our world, hiding in plain sight.

# Mysteries of the Hayride: The Haunting of the Farmland

In the rural heartland of Ohio lies the small town of Evermore, home to the vast Bennett Family Farm. This tranquil agricultural haven is known for its annual Halloween hayride, a beloved tradition that brings joy to both locals and visitors. Yet, beneath the innocent charm of this hayride, there exists an eerie mystery that unfolds every Halloween, transforming the jolly ride into a chilling journey into the spectral realm.

The tales of these paranormal experiences piqued my curiosity. As a paranormal investigator, I was eager to explore this uncharted territory and understand the spectral phenomena associated with the hayride. So, in late October, I found myself on the Bennett Farm, waiting for the sun to set and the haunting to begin.

The Bennett Farm was a picturesque setting, with sprawling fields, vibrant pumpkin patches, and a timeless charm. But as dusk fell, the pastoral beauty gave way to an uneasy stillness, setting the stage for the annual Halloween hayride.

Seated on a bale of hay, with the crisp autumn air brushing against my face, I joined the excited families for the ride. As the tractor rumbled into motion, we set off into the moonlit fields. The first half of the ride was an enjoyable journey, complete with tales of local lore and history shared by our guide.

However, as we ventured farther into the farmland, the atmosphere started to change. A sudden chill permeated the air, and the jovial laughter and chatter of the passengers started to dwindle. Then, out of nowhere, I saw it – an apparition.

It materialised by the edge of the field, its form pale and

flickering in the moonlight. It stood there, watching the hayride pass by, an ethereal figure lost in time. The apparition vanished as swiftly as it had appeared, leaving an eerie stillness in its wake.

But that was just the beginning. As the hayride continued, the spectral activity escalated. We saw more apparitions, each appearing to be stuck in a different time era. Some were dressed in traditional farming attire, while others wore clothes that looked like they belonged to the early 20th century. Each ghostly figure was absorbed in a spectral task, indifferent to the living world passing by them.

By the time the hayride reached the old Bennett family graveyard, the spectral activity had reached its peak. The air was thick with an otherworldly energy, and you could almost hear the faint echo of whispered conversations. Among the ancient gravestones, we saw spectral figures wandering aimlessly, their faces bearing a melancholic expression.

As the hayride concluded, the apparitions faded away, leaving behind an unsettling silence that hung over the farmland. The cheerful laughter and excitement of the passengers had given way to an awestruck silence. Each one of us had experienced something beyond the realm of the ordinary, a spectral journey that we would remember for years to come.

The Mysteries of the Hayride was a chilling exploration of the unknown, a haunting reminder of the thin veil that separates the living from the dead. The Bennett Farm was not just a place of agriculture; it was a spectral crossroads where the past and present coexisted, their stories intertwining in the fabric of reality. This eerie tale of the annual Halloween hayride is a testament to the mysteries that lurk in the most unsuspecting places, waiting for the veil to lift, revealing their ghostly narratives.

# Ghoul School: The Haunting of the Old Schoolhouse

Nestled in the rolling hills of Derbyshire, England, atop a desolate knoll, stands an imposing, forgotten relic of the past - the Old Ashbourne Schoolhouse. Abandoned for several decades, this haunting Victorian-era structure still bears the echo of the footsteps of children long gone, their voices hushed by the inexorable passage of time. Every Halloween, however, the schoolhouse seems to awaken from its slumber, as spectral residents come out to play, turning this forgotten building into a 'Ghoul School.'

As a seasoned paranormal investigator, the whispers of spectral activities around the Old Ashbourne Schoolhouse intrigued me. Thus, as October's chill started settling in, I found myself in Derbyshire, standing before the ivy-encrusted schoolhouse, its darkened windows mirroring the moon's eerie glow. I could feel an anticipatory chill in the air, an unseen welcoming committee of spectral students awaiting the evening bell.

As darkness fell, the desolation of the schoolhouse grew eerier. The hoot of an owl, the rustling of leaves under an invisible wind, the faint sound of the rusted weather vane turning atop the turret-like tower, every sound echoed the mysteries the schoolhouse held within its cold stone walls.

With the digital recorder in my hand and a flashlight as my guide, I pushed open the creaking wooden doors and entered the schoolhouse. The interior was a time capsule - old wooden desks arranged neatly, the blackboard still covered in dusty chalk residue, and a globe that had long stopped spinning.

The air was thick with the silence of a place long forgotten, yet as the night deepened, this silence began to fill with soft echoes from the past. The air grew colder, and an electrifying buzz of energy swept through the room. A spectral hum of childish laughter resonated from the corners of the classroom, and I felt a ghostly presence among the rows of old desks.

In the corner of my eye, I caught a fleeting glimpse of a little girl in a Victorian dress. She seemed focused on an unseen teacher at the front of the classroom, her face alight with curiosity and concentration. Just as quickly as she appeared, she faded into the dimly lit room, leaving a lingering chill in her wake.

As I continued my exploration, I saw more apparitions. They seemed to relive their past, stuck in a timeless loop, oblivious to my presence. The spectral boys played a game of marbles, their laughter ringing in my ears, and a young teacher spectre pointing to the faded blackboard, her mouth moving in an eternal lesson.

As the bewitching hour approached, I heard the faint chime of a school bell. The spectral hustle and bustle increased; it was as if the old schoolhouse was alive once again, its spectral residents busy in their eternal routine. But the climax of the night came with the appearance of the headmaster. Dressed in a faded suit, carrying a cane, he walked down the aisle, inspecting his eternal classroom, his spectral gaze resting momentarily on me, before he faded away.

I left the schoolhouse as dawn was breaking, the echo of the spectral school bell still ringing in my ears. The night at the Old Ashbourne Schoolhouse had been an intense spectral journey. It was a haunting reminder that the past continues to live in places we've forgotten, its residents waiting for Halloween to tell their tales, transforming the old schoolhouse into a Ghoul School.

These spectral inhabitants, locked in their timeless routine, gave a voice to the history of the old schoolhouse. Their presence was not malevolent, but a poignant echo of a time gone by. The old Ashbourne Schoolhouse on Halloween night serves as a spectral classroom for those willing to learn about life, time, and the everlasting echo of the past.

So, dear reader, let's keep turning the pages, keep

exploring, for the world of the paranormal is vast and filled with stories that defy our understanding of reality. And as we delve deeper, we might just find that the line between our world and theirs is as thin as a schoolhouse wall.

# Eerie Evenings at the Costume Ball: The Phantom Dancer

In the heart of Birmingham, England, an annual tradition was eagerly awaited by the residents. Every Halloween, the grand Aston Hall, a shining gem of the city's historic district, played host to the annual Halloween Costume Ball. But for those in the know, the ball promised more than just an evening of costumed revelry; it also beckoned an ethereal guest who danced with the living only on this one mystical night.

I had heard tales of the Phantom Dancer, an entity said to appear every Halloween at the Wentworth Mansion. Intrigued, I booked my ticket to Birmingham. On a mild

October evening, dressed in my best costume, I joined the throng of revellers eager for an evening of dancing and potential encounters with the otherworldly.

Stepping into Aston Hall was like being transported back in time. The grand ballroom, aglow with golden light from ornate chandeliers, buzzed with anticipation. Elegant costumes filled the room - knights and princesses, witches and warlocks, vintage figures from every era. But one spectral figure was yet to make an appearance: the Phantom Dancer.

As the clock struck nine, the grand orchestra began to play, filling the room with melodies from a bygone era. I stationed myself near the ballroom's entrance, hoping to catch a glimpse of the spectral dancer. An hour passed, then two. Nothing unusual happened.

Just as I was beginning to doubt the validity of the tales, the atmosphere in the room began to change. The music faltered, the temperature dropped, and a sense of anticipation filled the air. From the corner of my eye, I noticed a movement at the entrance of the ballroom. A figure had appeared, a woman in a Victorian-era ball gown, her face obscured by a feathered mask. She moved with an ethereal grace, drawing the gaze of every person in the room.

There was something otherworldly about her presence. The figure seemed semi-transparent, and she moved as though floating. A hushed silence fell over the room as the crowd parted, leaving the dance floor empty for the spectral dancer.

She moved towards the centre of the room, her flowing gown leaving no impression on the polished floorboards. The orchestra, as if on cue, began a haunting waltz. The Phantom Dancer began to sway to the music, her movements fluid and graceful. It was as if time had stopped, the entire room entranced by this spectral presence.

I watched, utterly fascinated. It was a sight to behold, a step back in time, and a dance with the unknown. The Phantom Dancer twirled, dipped, and swayed as if locked in a dance with an unseen partner. Her spectral figure glided across the room in perfect synchrony with the music, an ethereal dance that left the onlookers spellbound.

As the waltz neared its end, the Phantom Dancer seemed to grow fainter, her figure becoming translucent. And with the last note of the waltz, she vanished, leaving an eerie chill in her wake. The crowd stood in stunned silence, having witnessed something that blurred the line between the earthly and the spectral.

The rest of the evening was filled with hushed whispers and wide-eyed recollections of the spectral dance. As I left the ballroom in the early hours of the morning, I couldn't help but feel a sense of awe. The Phantom Dancer had brought the past to the present in an elegant dance, reminding us of the thin veil that separates our world from the spectral realm.

Experiencing the Phantom Dancer's spectral waltz was an encounter I would never forget. It was a testament to the mysteries that the world of the paranormal held, an example of how the living and the dead could intertwine on a night when the veil between worlds was thinnest.

The Halloween Costume Ball at Aston Hall served as a yearly reminder that we share our world with entities beyond our comprehension, beings that dance on the edge of our reality. And on that Halloween night, as the spectral waltz played out in front of a crowd of onlookers, we all became part of a dance that transcended time, a dance with the spectral realm.

As we turn the page onto the next story, remember this: there is more to our world than meets the eye, more to uncover, more to explore. And as we delve into the mysteries of the spectral realm, we realise that perhaps, just perhaps, the dance with the unknown is one that never truly ends.

# Bone-Chilling Bonfire: The Legend of the Campsite

Perched at the edge of the woods, nestled against the backdrop of the rugged Colorado mountains, was the campsite that bore the eerie legend of the Bone-Chilling Bonfire. Every year, a group of friends ventured out to this campsite for their annual Halloween camping trip. And every year, as the flames of the bonfire rose against the inky black canvas of the night sky, they would experience a series of paranormal events that tested their scepticism and courage.

I first heard about this legend from one of the campers, an old friend. The tales of apparitions, eerie whispers, and unexplained phenomena were too intriguing to ignore. I knew I had to experience it for myself. And so, I found myself accompanying my friend and his group on their annual Halloween trip, armed with my investigation equipment and an insatiable curiosity.

The campsite was a picture of idyllic serenity when we arrived on a crisp October afternoon. The riot of fall colours provided a beautiful contrast to the imposing mountains and clear, blue skies. Yet, I couldn't shake off an uneasy feeling, a subtle undercurrent that hinted at the hidden secrets of this place.

As dusk fell, we gathered around a clearing to build the bonfire. The crackling flames provided a comforting warmth against the chilly mountain air. Ghost stories began to flow, each tale more frightening than the last. Yet, they all paled in comparison to what we were about to experience.

As the clock neared midnight, the atmosphere around us started to change. The wind howled through the trees, the temperature dropped, and an eerie silence fell over the campsite. We huddled closer to the fire, anticipation and fear prickling at the back of our necks. As if on cue, we heard a soft whisper floating on the wind. A chill ran down my spine as I strained to listen. The whisper grew louder, morphing into a chorus of spectral voices that seemed to surround us.

Suddenly, the bonfire blazed up, the flames reaching an unnatural height. The spectral voices became a panicked cacophony. The faces around me mirrored my terror. We were in the throes of something paranormal, something beyond our comprehension.

Just when we thought things couldn't get more terrifying, a figure emerged from the bonfire. It was a spectral apparition, an ethereal figure engulfed in flames. It had no discernible features, only a pair of glowing eyes that held us in a hypnotic trance. The figure hovered in front of us for a few minutes that felt like an eternity, its eyes scanning each one of us.

The spectral figure slowly receded back into the fire, the flames engulfing it completely. The voices faded away, the wind quieted down, and the temperature slowly started to rise. As quickly as it had started, the paranormal activity ceased.

We sat in stunned silence, our minds struggling to process what we had just witnessed. The legend of the Bone-Chilling Bonfire was not just a legend; it was a bone-chilling reality.

In the days that followed, I went over the recordings and the data I had collected. The temperature drops, the voices, and the apparition all pointed towards a strong spectral presence. Whatever entity haunted the campsite, it was powerful and possibly tied to the land.

Experiencing the Bone-Chilling Bonfire was an unforgettable encounter with the paranormal. It was a chilling reminder of the unknown entities that exist on the fringes of our world, their stories etched into the very fabric of the places they inhabit.

As we move deeper into the mysteries of the paranormal world, we discover that even places of beauty and tranquillity can harbour chilling secrets. Our world is indeed a tapestry of countless stories and experiences, some seen, many unseen, and it's only when we step out of our comfort zones do we truly begin to understand its complexities. And so, the journey continues, leading us to realms unexplored, guiding us through the vast expanse of the unknown.

# The Uninvited Guest: Haunting of the Halloween Feast

Nestled within the historic district of Savannah, Georgia, stands the Majestic House - a grand manor with an imposing façade that held an age-old tale of a spectral uninvited guest. Once the residence of a wealthy merchant, the house had been handed down generations and was now home to the Bellington family, who had been experiencing unsettling occurrences each Halloween night during their traditional feast.

Having caught wind of the rumours circulating about the peculiar incidents that transpired within the house during this spectral season, my intrigue was piqued. With a keen desire to unearth the truth behind these tales, I accepted the Bellingtons' invitation to attend their Halloween feast, equipped with my tools and a burning determination to document the events of the night.

The evening of October 31st found the Majestic House bathed in a dim, warm glow, with pumpkins lined along the driveway and the faint echo of laughter wafting from inside. A sense of anticipation hung in the air, punctuated by an undercurrent of apprehension as the grand clock in the hallway struck six, marking the beginning of the feast.

The dining room was a splendid sight with a long oak table laden with a variety of dishes, illuminated by the soft light of antique chandeliers. The feast commenced, a time-honoured tradition passed down generations of the Bellington lineage. Yet, an air of unease was palpable, a stark contrast to the warm, inviting ambiance.

As the night wore on, the atmosphere began to shift. The laughter and jovial conversation tapered off, replaced by an eerie silence. A chill coursed through the room, causing the flames in the fireplace to flicker. The grandfather clock chimed ominously, the resonance seeming to reverberate through the entire house. The haunted hour was upon us.

The room grew cold and still. The fire in the hearth flickered and dimmed, casting long, distorted shadows that danced eerily on the ancient wallpaper. The air became dense with a bone-chilling intensity that seemed to constrict the very breath from our lungs. Suddenly, a gust of wind swept through the room, snuffing out the candles and plunging us into darkness.

With a loud creak, the dining room door swung open, seemingly of its own accord. A harsh, cold wind howled through the open doorway, causing the remaining embers in the fireplace to flare momentarily. That's when we saw it. In the ghostly glow of the dying firelight, a spectral figure stood in the doorway. It was ethereal and shimmering, a ghostly silhouette backlit by the pale moonlight filtering in from the hallway windows.

A collective gasp echoed through the room. The spectral

figure moved towards the head of the table, its movements slow and deliberate. As it reached the vacant chair at the end of the table, it paused, then slowly sat down. The room fell into a stunned silence, every pair of eyes fixated on the spectral entity.

The figure looked around the room, its gaze lingering on each one of us before focusing on the feast spread out on the table. It reached out, its translucent hand passing through the dishes and silverware, causing a chilling ripple to pass through the room.

For what felt like an eternity, we watched in frozen horror as the spectral figure carried out its eerie ritual. And then, as suddenly as it had appeared, it faded away, the temperature in the room gradually returning to normal and the oppressive atmosphere lifting.

In the following days, I combed through the data I'd collected. The sudden temperature drops, the spectral figure, and the physical interaction all pointed to a strong paranormal presence.

The "Uninvited Guest of the Halloween Feast," as I've come to call it, remains one of the most profound paranormal experiences I've had. While we may not have understood its purpose, or why it chose to appear during the Halloween feast, the encounter was a powerful reminder of the thin veil that separates our world from the unknown.

Each Halloween, as families gather around their tables to celebrate, I'm reminded of the spectral figure at the Majestic House. And I wonder if perhaps, in some way, it was also trying to be a part of something it once knew, a ghostly echo from a past long gone, forever bound to the haunting refrain of All Hallows' Eve.

# Specter of the Scarecrow: Haunted Fields of October

The picturesque town of Bitterroot, nestled deep within the heart of Idaho, is known for its lush farmlands and rustic charm. Here, amidst the golden fields and under the vast expanse of the autumn sky, I was introduced to a haunting tale. A tale that had woven itself into the very fabric of the town's lore, a story of a scarecrow in the wheat fields that turned into a spectral beacon each Halloween night.

The Benson farm, a large stretch of land dominated by waving wheat and cornfields, stood on the outskirts of the town. The Bensons had been farmers for generations, tilling the land, sowing the seeds, and reaping the golden bounty that Mother Earth bestowed upon them. But their humble life was not without its unusual and chilling occurrences.

Every Halloween, a scarecrow, affectionately named Old Rags by the Bensons, stood sentinel in the fields. Dressed in worn-out overalls, a straw hat, and a stitched burlap sack for a face, Old Rags was a typical scarecrow in every way - save for the eerie happenings that were said to occur every All Hallows Eve.

On the night of October 31st, as the tale went, the usually benign figure of the scarecrow would become a conduit for an unseen, vengeful entity, sending a wave of inexplicable terror through the entire farm. The intriguing aspect of this paranormal phenomenon caught my attention, and thus, I found myself in Bitterroot, invited by the Bensons to experience the eerie spectacle first-hand.

Halloween night arrived, bringing with it a chilling wind that swept through the wheat fields. As the sun set and shadows began to stretch across the land, a sense of heightened anticipation set in. Dusk gave way to the darkness, and the silhouetted figure of Old Rags stood out starkly against the moonlit field.

With my tools set up and the Bensons huddled inside their farmhouse, we watched as the clock struck midnight, marking the onset of the supernatural phenomena that were said to unfold.

As the twelfth stroke echoed into the silent night, an unnerving calm descended. Suddenly, a cold gust of wind swept through the fields, causing the wheat to rustle and sway as if in response to an unseen command. The usually lifeless form of Old Rags twitched, drawing a gasp from everyone present.

What happened next was beyond comprehension. The scarecrow seemed to come alive. It shook violently as if gripped by an unseen force. Its previously limp straw arms began to flail, and an eerie glow emanated from its burlap face, illuminating the field with an otherworldly light.

Then, the disembodied voice echoed through the night, a deep, resonant tone that was both chilling and sorrowful. It spoke of lost love and vengeance, a tale of a farmer betrayed and a spirit unable to find rest.

The spectral activity continued until the first light of dawn appeared on the horizon. As the sun rose, the unnatural glow faded from Old Rags, and it became once again, a regular scarecrow, a silent sentinel amidst the wheat.

In the days that followed, I analysed the data I had gathered that night. The recordings, the fluctuations in temperature, and the electromagnetic readings all pointed to a significant paranormal presence centred around the scarecrow.

The "Specter of the Scarecrow," as I have come to term this case, remains one of the most unusual and chilling encounters of my paranormal career. It serves as a stark reminder of the mysteries that our world holds, often hidden in the most unexpected of places - and in this case, embodied in the straw-filled sentinel of the Benson's wheat field each Halloween.

Is the scarecrow indeed a spectral conduit for a vengeful spirit? Or is it merely a part of the town's lore, spun into a chilling Halloween tale? The truth remains as elusive as the spirit itself, hidden within the rustling wheat fields under the October moon, forever bound to the spectral figure of Old Rags on All Hallows' Eve.

# Banshee's Wails: The Haunting Sounds of All Hallow's Eve

Nestled along the rocky coastline of Maine, the quaint fishing town of Point Harbor is steeped in a rich maritime history and old-world charm. However, this coastal town is not just known for its picturesque lighthouses and delectable clam chowder. It also carries with it a chilling folklore, a haunting siren song that emanates every Halloween night from the depths of the sea.

Local residents have reported hearing blood-curdling wails echoing over the waves. Some claim it is the wind, others, the cries of a lost ship, but most residents attribute it to a far more supernatural source: a banshee. These tales led me to this maritime hamlet, intrigued by the idea of a spectral siren haunting the coast on Halloween.

As October drew to a close, the town's anticipation and anxiety grew. It wasn't just the salty sea air that was charged; it was the very atmosphere of Point Harbor that carried an undercurrent of apprehension. The townsfolk braced themselves for the eerie cries they had come to associate with All Hallows' Eve.

On Halloween night, the quaint town was shrouded in an ethereal fog, the full moon casting long, spectral shadows on the cobblestone streets. The waves crashed rhythmically against the shore, the only sound breaking the silence of the cold night.

As I took my place among the local crowd that had gathered by the lighthouse, I felt a shiver of anticipation. Armed with a digital recorder and a healthy dose of scepticism, I waited for the stroke of midnight, the hour at which the spectral cries were reportedly heard.

The bell in the town square tolled the midnight hour, its sonorous chime echoing into the silence. Then, just as the last echo faded, it started: a haunting, mournful wail that froze the blood in our veins. The sound seemed to rise from the ocean, floating over the waves, filling the air with an unmistakable tone of lament and sorrow.

Each wail was more heart-wrenching than the last, echoing across the vast expanse of the sea, creating an unsettling symphony that penetrated the fog and filled the night. The eerie cries resonated in the silence, their intensity fluctuating with the ebb and flow of the waves.

With every fibre of my being focused on the spectral serenade, I started recording, hoping to capture the paranormal phenomenon in its purest form. I noted the reactions of the townsfolk around me, the visible fear, the collective shiver that ran through the crowd with each piercing wail.

As suddenly as it had started, the haunting cries ceased, leaving behind a deafening silence and an air of melancholy.

The only sound that remained was the lapping of the waves against the shore.

In the days that followed, I checked my recordings, my mind filled with the haunting echoes of the banshee's wails. The sounds I captured didn't match any known animal or natural phenomenon, adding more credibility to the townsfolk's claims.

The 'Banshee's Wails' of Point Harbor left a lasting impression, not just on the digital files of my recorder, but etched into my memory. This Halloween haunting, this eerie siren song of sorrow, was a chilling reminder of the thin veil that separates the living from the dead, a veil that seemingly becomes translucent on the eve of All Hallows'.

The wailing banshee of Point Harbor has become a part of the town's identity, a chilling nocturne that sings the symphony of the supernatural each Halloween night. A haunted melody that is, in itself, a siren call to those of us who seek to understand the mysteries that lurk in the shadows of the unseen. A reminder that the paranormal isn't always just in the things we see, but also in the sounds we hear, especially on a cold, foggy Halloween night by the sea.

# Restless Shadows: The Spirits of the Haunted Hollow

In the heart of Massachusetts lies a serene town named Ashfield, known for its picturesque landscapes and scenic trails that lead into a peaceful hollow. However, this tranquillity is only surface deep, for when the leaves start changing colours and the air turns crisp, the hollow reveals its eerie secret. As All Hallows' Eve draws near, the hollow transforms into a spectral theatre, presenting a spectacle of restless shadows.

As a paranormal investigator, I was drawn to Ashfield by these accounts of spectral shadows seen by the townsfolk each Halloween. Their stories spoke of flickering figures dancing in the moonlight, ghostly apparitions flitting amongst the trees, casting an otherworldly pallor over the hollow.

When I arrived in late October, Ashfield was a quaint picture of autumn charm. The vibrant hues of fall leaves provided a stark contrast to the tales of spectral shadows I was there to investigate. I was led to the heart of the hollow, a secluded grove surrounded by towering trees. This spot was reported to be the epicentre of the shadowy activity.

As I settled in the hollow on the eve of Halloween, the last of the day's sunlight waned, giving way to a thick blanket of darkness, only broken by the silver glow of the moon. The hollow was quiet, save for the distant hoot of an owl and the rustling of leaves carried by the wind. I readied my equipment, waiting for the spectral dance to begin.

As the clock neared midnight, I noticed a distinct change in the air, an unexplainable chill that seemed to seep from the earth itself. The tranquillity of the hollow was replaced with a palpable sense of expectancy. Then, as the church bell in the distance chimed twelve, the performance began.

Shadows detached from the dark recesses of the trees, taking on a life of their own. They flickered in the moonlight, growing in intensity, their ethereal forms stretching and swirling, dancing in a silent ballet. A spectral waltz performed by unseen dancers, their ghostly silhouettes illuminated by the ethereal moonlight.

The shadows moved with purpose, twirling around the hollow, giving an impression of past lives reliving their moments. One shadow in particular caught my attention. It was distinct and more defined than the others, seemingly aware of my presence. It floated towards me, its form flickering like a candle's flame, then extended what appeared to be a hand.

Hesitant, yet driven by my quest to understand the unknown, I reached out. The moment I made contact, a cold shock spread up my arm. A barrage of images flooded my mind, echoes of joy, sorrow, love, and loss. It was as if I was experiencing the shadow's memories, its life and beyond.

The exchange lasted for a brief moment before the spectral

figure retreated, blending back into the whirling mass of shadows. Left in a state of awe, I realised I had experienced a direct communication with these spectral entities, something far beyond any regular paranormal encounter.

The dance of the shadows continued until the first light of dawn started to filter through the trees. As if on cue, the shadowy figures retreated, merging back into the shadows from where they emerged. The hollow fell quiet once more, returning to its peaceful state as if the spectral spectacle of the night was nothing more than an illusion.

In the days that followed, I reviewed my notes, the memory of the ethereal dance forever imprinted in my mind. I realised the shadowy figures were not restless spirits but echoes of past inhabitants of Ashfield, their life energies imprinted in the hollow. Their spectral dance was not one of haunting but a reminder of their existence, a testament to their lives that once were.

The Halloween night in Ashfield's hollow provided a unique perspective on spectral encounters, one that added depth to my understanding of the paranormal. As I left the town, I carried with me the memory of the spectral shadows, a reminder of the lives that once graced the hollow, and the dance they perform each Halloween, under the watchful gaze of the moon.

# Halloween Hex: The Curious Case of the Cursed Family

The White Family had resided in the town of Cedar Creek, Oregon, for generations. They were known for their prominence in local history and their stunning family estate, which stood atop a hill, overlooking the entire town. However, an unusual rumour surrounded the family - a rumour of an ancestral curse that was said to awaken every Halloween. As a paranormal investigator, I was drawn to this tale, and it wasn't long before I found myself on a flight to Oregon to delve into the mystery of the White Family's Halloween Hex.

Upon my arrival, I was greeted by Thomas White, the current head of the family. Thomas was a middle-aged man, with a warm smile but an unmistakable shadow of worry in his eyes. Over a cup of tea, he spoke of the unusual happenings that plagued their family every Halloween. He described strange noises echoing throughout their ancestral home, objects mysteriously moving, lights flickering, and a general sense of unease that settled over the family as Halloween approached. These occurrences seemed to have increased in intensity with each passing year.

Thomas's story piqued my interest, and I was eager to delve deeper into the mystery. I asked him about the origin of the alleged curse. Thomas explained that the curse dated back to his great-great-grandfather, Harold White. Harold had been a ruthless businessman who, according to local lore, had wronged a woman believed to be a witch. In her fury, the woman had supposedly placed a curse on Harold and his descendants, a curse that would make itself known each All Hallows' Eve.

With this information, I began my investigation. In the days leading up to Halloween, I spent countless hours in the White family library, digging into old records, family documents, and diaries. I found mention of Harold's misdeeds and the curse in an old, worn-out diary belonging to Harold himself. The entries confirmed the oral history and also revealed a sense of remorse in Harold's later life. But was this remorse enough to bring an end to the alleged curse?

As Halloween approached, the atmosphere in the White residence grew tense. The usual laughter and conversation were replaced by apprehensive glances and hushed whispers. As October 31st dawned, I readied my equipment, eager to document any spectral activity.

With the falling of dusk, the air inside the White mansion became heavy, as if charged with anticipation. The house seemed to take on a life of its own, the halls echoing with strange whispers, and lights flickering inexplicably. I could see the family's fears were not unfounded. Their apprehension was mirrored in the gathering storm clouds outside, casting long, ominous shadows throughout the mansion.

As midnight approached, the strange occurrences escalated. I witnessed a heavy grandfather clock, which had been stationary for years, suddenly start ticking. Family portraits hanging on the walls inexplicably tilted, and the scent of roses, Harold White's favourite flower, filled the air. The spectral happenings seemed intent on making the presence known, yet there was no sense of malevolence. It was as if the spirit wanted to communicate something.

Seizing this opportunity, I decided to attempt a séance. Gathering the family in the main hall, we sat around a table, our hands joined. As I began the séance, a cold wind swept through the room, causing the candles to flicker. A sense of anticipation filled the air.

Slowly, a presence seemed to join us. A spectral figure materialised at the head of the table - a man, his apparition bearing a striking resemblance to the portrait of Harold White hanging in the hallway. The air around us became heavy with emotion. The spirit of Harold White had a sorrowful air to it, his eyes filled with regret.

In the eerily silent room, a voice echoed, seeming to come from Harold's apparition. It spoke of regret, of actions taken in anger and the consequences that had followed. The voice asked for forgiveness from his descendants, and as the words faded, so did Harold's spirit. The room seemed lighter, the previously flickering lights steady, and the scent of roses slowly faded away.

The Halloween Hex of the White family was not a curse but a plea for forgiveness from a remorseful spirit. This Halloween, Harold White's spirit had found the redemption it sought, bringing an end to the century-old Halloween Hex. The White family was left in stunned silence, their ancestral curse lifted, replaced by a tale of remorse, redemption, and forgiveness.

As the sun rose on November 1st, the White family home felt different - warmer and more peaceful. Their Halloween Hex was now a tale they would recount as a story of their ancestor's redemption. For me, this case underscored the idea that not all hauntings are malicious. Some spirits may just be trapped, burdened by their past actions, seeking solace, and a chance to correct their wrongs.

The Halloween Hex of the White Family served as a stark reminder that our actions echo into eternity, influencing not only our lives but potentially the lives of generations that follow. As a paranormal investigator, I find solace in helping those, both living and dead, to find peace, and in the case of the White family's Halloween Hex, that peace was finally attained.

# Frightful Flickers: The Ghost of the Old Movie Theatre

Nestled in the heart of Dunwich, Massachusetts, the vintage 'Starlight Cinema' had been a local landmark since the 1940s. In recent years, the theatre had earned a chilling reputation for being haunted, and not just by celluloid phantoms. Residents whispered about the spectral cinephile, an entity that seemed to emerge specifically around the cinema's Halloween horror movie marathon. As a fan of both the paranormal and classic horror films, I couldn't resist the allure of the Starlight Cinema. My investigations led me to Dunwich in the cool autumn, just in time for the Halloween season.

Upon arrival, I met the theatre's current owner, a burly but kind-hearted man named Henry. A film enthusiast himself, he had taken over the dilapidated theatre a few years ago, bringing it back to its former glory. When I inquired about the spectral cinephile, Henry shared several eerie tales. Employees reported unexplained phenomena—projectors starting by themselves, ghostly applause heard from the empty theatre, and an inexplicable figure spotted in the vintage red velvet seats.

Henry's accounts sparked my curiosity, and I requested permission to investigate the theatre. He agreed, on the condition that I would share my findings. Eager to uncover the mystery, I delved into the theatre's history, and one story caught my attention: the tale of Oliver "Ollie" Sullivan, an avid movie-goer, and a cinema employee during the theatre's early years. Tragically, Ollie had died in an accident in the theatre. The timeline fit perfectly with the theatre's ghostly activities, as most reports began surfacing around the time of Ollie's unfortunate demise.

On the eve of Halloween, the Starlight Cinema was set to kick off its horror marathon. My equipment was set up throughout the theatre—voice recorders, cameras, infrared sensors—all in an attempt to capture any sign of spectral activity. As the night's first flick, a vintage horror gem, began, I felt a sudden drop in temperature, a classic sign of a spectral presence. An infrared camera showed an odd distortion in one corner of the theatre—a figure materialised in one of the seats, a spectral silhouette, its gaze fixed on the silver screen.

Throughout the movie, I could hear ghostly shuffling and the faint sound of whispered commentary, echoing the classic dialogue. As the final credits rolled, I distinctly heard a spectral applause, followed by the hushed whisper, "Bravo!" An EVP (Electronic Voice Phenomenon) device picked up these sounds, confirming my experiences. A spectral cinephile was indeed attending the Halloween marathon.

In the dim glow of the projector's light, I attempted to communicate with the spirit. Using a spirit box, a device used for contacting spirits through radio frequencies, I asked, "Are you Ollie?" A static-filled moment later, a male voice echoed through the spirit box, "Yes."

The dialogue with Ollie was surreal. He spoke about his love for cinema, the magic of the silver screen, and his regret of not being able to enjoy the world of film due to his untimely demise. The spectral cinephile seemed harmless, his afterlife intertwined with his passion for movies.

With Ollie's confirmation, the haunting of the Starlight Cinema was no longer a mere local legend but a confirmed spectral phenomena—a testament to one man's undying love for cinema. I presented my findings to Henry, who was moved by the story.

That Halloween, as audiences shrieked in delightful terror during the horror marathon, a spectral film lover was among them, relishing the magic of the movies. The Starlight Cinema's haunting added a new layer to its rich history, and it continued to welcome patrons—both living and deceased—to its annual Halloween horror movie marathon. The Frightful Flickers of the old Starlight Cinema served as a poignant reminder of the imprints we leave behind and the passions that can transcend mortality.

# Midnight in the Library: The Haunting of the Halloween Book Club

The ancient city of York in the United Kingdom is no stranger to ghost stories. With its rich history stretching back to Roman times, through the Viking invasions, mediaeval era, and into the present, it is regarded as one of the most haunted cities in the world. Among its winding cobbled streets and within its majestic stone walls, each building seems to have a spectral tale to tell.

Perhaps the most fascinating of these tales originates from the York Central Library, a grand, historic building of gothic architecture that looms silently over Museum Street. Its imposing stone exterior, with intricate carvings and tall, mullioned windows, whispers of the countless stories contained within its walls. In the heart of this architectural treasure, the local book club conducts its monthly meetings.

Every Halloween, the book club would gather in the main reading room, a cavernous space with an ornate ceiling that stretched high overhead. Massive bookcases lined the walls, filled with timeworn tomes and more recent additions. On this particular Halloween, they decided to read Mary Shelley's "Frankenstein," an apt choice given the chilling atmosphere that the season brought with it.

As the clock struck midnight, the only light in the reading room was the soft, warm glow of the antique table lamp around which the book club members were gathered. One by one, they took turns reading passages from the haunting tale, their voices echoing softly in the hush of the library. As they delved deeper into the night and the story, an inexplicable chill seemed to fill the room.

Emma, a longstanding member of the club and a firm believer in the paranormal, was the first to notice it. A sudden drop in temperature, the hairs on the back of her neck standing up, a feeling of being watched. Emma's heartbeat quickened as she looked around the room. She noticed that the others seemed to be experiencing the same sensations, their faces pale under the dim light.

Soon, they began to hear faint whispers filling the room, soft at first, then growing louder. The whispers seemed to emanate from the old books themselves, as though the very stories they held were seeping out into the room. The chilling sensation deepened, and the air in the room seemed to thicken. A hushed unease spread among the club members.

Then, with an abruptness that made everyone jump, a book flew off a shelf on the far side of the room. It landed with a loud thump in the centre of the room, lying open on the floor. Everyone stared at the book, stunned into silence. Emma, after taking a deep breath, walked over to pick it up. It was an old diary dated back to the 1800s, belonging to a former librarian known as Miss Abigail Harkness.

She skimmed the pages, her eyes widening as she read aloud entries that documented strange occurrences in the library - whispers heard in the dead of night, books mysteriously displaced, sightings of a spectral figure among the stacks. The very last entry, dated October 31st, 1895, described an encounter with what Abigail believed was the ghost of a former scholar, an ardent bibliophile who frequented the library and had died tragically young.

The realisation set in among the book club members - they were not alone. The library, with its ancient knowledge, appeared to house a spectral presence. A silence fell over the room, each person contemplating the eerie events. The haunting of the Halloween Book Club was a chilling testament to the age-old adage that truth could indeed be stranger than fiction. With an air of respect for the resident ghost, the group packed up their belongings and left the library, leaving only the soft whispers of spectral stories behind.

Every Halloween since, they have gathered in the reading room, their midnight book club embracing the haunting as a part of their tradition. Even today, if one dares to visit the York Central Library on Halloween night, they may just catch the faint echo of whispers, and feel the spectral scholar's presence in the hallowed hall of stories. The tale of the haunting of the Halloween Book Club endures, adding another spectral layer to the ghostly tapestry of York's history.

# Witching Hour Whispers: The Voices of the Haunted Clock Tower

In the historic township of Ashford nestled deep within the verdant English countryside, the century-old clock tower stood as a resolute symbol of time. It had faithfully ticked away the seconds, minutes, and hours of countless generations, overseeing years of joy, sorrow, birth, and death. The towering structure, with its weathered sandstone bricks and intricate gilded hands, was the heart of Ashford, a silent guardian marking the passage of time.

Yet, the clock tower held a secret. Every year, as October rolled around, the townsfolk would recall hushed tales about the strange occurrences surrounding the clock tower.

For you see, on the eve of Halloween, the clock, known to be unfailingly accurate, would strike thirteen times instead of the customary twelve at the stroke of midnight. This, in itself, was an oddity that was both peculiar and unsettling. But there was something more - whispers, faint and eerie, echoing through the winds, originating from the tower itself.

On this particular Halloween, a group of Ashford's curious and brave - or perhaps foolish - decided to investigate the haunted clock tower. Armed with nothing but their courage, flashlights, and a few rumours about Ashford's past, they ventured into the darkened streets, their destination looming high against the starless night. The wind howled through the cobblestone streets, whispering ancient secrets and forgotten tales.

As they reached the tower, the usually friendly and comforting tick-tock of the clock echoed ominously through the night. A shiver of anticipation ran down their spines. Taking a deep breath, they opened the heavy wooden door leading to the clock tower's heart and began their steep ascent up the spiral staircase.

The deeper they ventured, the colder and more foreboding the atmosphere became. The air was heavy with dust and the scent of aged wood, but beneath that was something else, something they couldn't quite place - an otherworldly musk that permeated their senses and made the hairs on the back of their necks stand on end. As the midnight hour drew nearer, the tower seemed to awaken, its atmosphere crackling with unseen energy.

Finally, they reached the clock's mechanism - a marvel of engineering that had stood the test of time. But as they stared at the intricate gears and springs, they could feel a presence, an invisible force surrounding them. The air grew colder still, and an eerie silence enveloped the room. The tick-tock of the clock grew louder, each beat resonating in their chests. The anticipation was nearly unbearable.

Then, as the long hand joined the short one at the top of the clock face, marking the midnight hour, a hush fell over the group. The clock began to chime - once, twice, thrice - the sound was deafening in the silence of the room. They counted each strike, hearts pounding in rhythm with the clock - nine, ten, eleven, twelve.

But then, in defiance of logic and reason, a thirteenth strike rang out, reverberating through the tower and shaking them to their very cores.

As the echo of the thirteenth strike faded, an ethereal whispering began. It was soft at first, a mere rustling like leaves in the wind, but it grew louder and more insistent. The voices seemed to be coming from the very walls of the tower, whispering tales of forgotten times, ancient battles, love lost, and the undying spirit of Ashford's ancestors. It was as if the tower itself was a vessel for the voices of the past, allowed to speak but once a year.

As quickly as it had begun, the whispering faded away, leaving the group in stunned silence. They looked at each other, wide-eyed and pale, their scepticism washed away by the undeniable reality they had witnessed. The haunted clock tower of Ashford was more than a legend; it was a spectral time capsule, a testament to the town's rich history and the timeless stories of its people.

With newfound respect and a touch of fear, they descended the staircase, leaving the tower to its eternal duty. They left with more than they had bargained for - a chilling experience, a story to tell, and a deeper connection with the town they called home.

From that Halloween night forward, the thirteenth strike of the Ashford clock tower was no longer met with fear but with reverent silence as the townsfolk listened to the whispers of their ancestors. It was a haunting yet oddly comforting tradition - a spectral link to their past, reminding them that while time marches forward, it never truly leaves behind the echoes of yesteryears.

# Cobweb Castle: The Haunted Halloween Tour

In the heart of the misty Scottish Highlands, perched atop a craggy hill and surrounded by a seemingly endless sea of heather, stood Cobweb Castle. A brooding edifice of towering turrets and imposing stone walls, the castle was as much a part of the wild landscape as the heather and the towering pine trees. Its legacy, woven into the fabric of Scottish history, was steeped in heroism, betrayal, love, and loss. Yet, its most enduring legend was one of ghostly apparitions and spectral cries in the night. Every Halloween, the castle's history was opened to the public with a grand tour, a blend of historical intrigue and terrifying encounters.

On this year's Halloween night, the moon hung low in the

sky, casting an eerie pallor over the Highland moors as visitors gathered at the castle's gate. A chill wind wove through the crowd, whispering tales of spectral knights and ghostly damsels. Dressed in layers of warm clothing with torches in hand, they were a motley group of thrill-seekers, history enthusiasts, and curious locals.

Guiding them through their nocturnal journey was Elder MacGregor, a wizened man with a mane of white hair and a booming voice that echoed through the castle halls. An authority on the castle's history and folklore, he was as much a part of the Halloween tour as the castle itself.

The tour began in the castle's grand foyer, a cavernous space adorned with the faded banners of noble families and the worn-out coats of arms of fallen knights. MacGregor's stories brought the history to life; tales of kings and queens, blood feuds, and lost treasures. As the group moved through the castle's stone corridors and winding staircases, the air grew colder, the shadows deeper. An unspoken tension built amongst the visitors as they ventured further into the castle.

The grand ballroom was next, a massive room with a soaring ceiling and grand chandeliers that now hung, abandoned, covered in years of cobwebs. Here, MacGregor recounted tales of grand celebrations, of laughter and music that filled the room. But as the wind howled against the castle's stone walls, the visitors could almost hear the faint strains of a ghostly melody, the whispers of a long-ago party.

In the royal chambers, a spectral queen was said to roam, forever looking for her lost love. As the visitors peered into the room, the air thick with anticipation, a sudden drop in temperature was palpable. A woman in the group gasped, swearing she saw a figure, ethereal and white, standing by the window.

The castle's haunting pinnacle, however, was the dungeon, a labyrinth of dark, damp cells deep beneath the castle. A place of torment and despair, the cries of its long-dead prisoners were said to echo through the stone halls on Halloween night. As they descended into the depths, the laughter and excited chatter died down, replaced by an uneasy silence.

In the near darkness, the flickering torchlight casting ominous shadows on the dungeon walls, MacGregor fell silent. His usually rambunctious demeanour was replaced by a sombre seriousness. He warned the group to stay close and listen carefully. At first, all they could hear was the distant dripping of water. But then, gradually, another sound emerged. A faint, drawn-out wailing echoed through the dungeon, chilling their blood and making their hairs stand on end.

Panic started to bubble amongst the group. The brave faces of thrill-seekers fell, replaced with wide-eyed fear. The haunting cries continued, the spectral sorrow reaching out from the past and gripping their hearts. It was a symphony of despair, a haunting testament to the castle's dark history. Even MacGregor, a seasoned historian, paled at the spectral sounds, the reality of the haunting more potent than he'd ever witnessed.

The spectral tour ended with heartbeats pounding in their

ears and a renewed respect for the castle's haunted inhabitants. The visitors emerged from the depths of Cobweb Castle shaken, their jovial anticipation replaced by a lingering fear and a sense of awe.

The haunted tour of Cobweb Castle was a Halloween tradition like no other, a night where history and the spectral world entwined. Each visitor left with a tale to tell, a personal encounter with the castle's spectral inhabitants. The ghostly echoes of the past lingered long after, reminding them of the enduring spirit of Cobweb Castle, forever rooted in the heart of the Scottish Highlands.

# Afterword

As I lay down my pen, having navigated through 26 chilling cases, a sense of profound reflection washes over me. Through the pages of "Haunted Halloween: 26 Chilling True Tales of Spooky October Nights and Paranormal Mysteries," I have led you, dear reader, into a world that exists alongside ours, often unseen, but always felt. The spectral realm, where time and space seem to twist and turn in ways our mortal minds find hard to grasp.

The journey began in the shadows of an ancient Victorian mansion, with an All Hallow's Eve that veered from festivity to terror. In sharing these cases, I sought not only to send shivers down your spine but to convey the haunted tapestry of human experiences and emotions that exist in these encounters. Fear and mystery, yes, but also wonder, sadness, curiosity, and at times, even warmth.

Throughout these narratives, from the unseen entity that lurks on Trick-or-Treat Street, to the spectral presence that haunts the candy factory every Halloween, we've walked through the thin veil separating the living from the dead. Each chapter was a plunge into the heart of a Halloween mystery, filled with eerie phenomena that piqued our intrigue and tested our courage.

We journeyed into the heart of the pumpkin patch, bathed in the light of the Harvest Moon, felt the jinx of the Jack-O'-Lantern in the chaos of a carving contest, and faced the haunting presence in a Halloween store. We watched the phantom march alone at a costume parade and caught glimpses of the witch of the Willow Woods.

You were there with me during the chilling séance in the graveyard and while unravelling the curse of a black cat on a suburban street. We ventured into an abandoned house besieged by an October poltergeist and felt the chill run down our spines in an apple orchard on Halloween. From the mysteries of the corn maze to the haunted farmland's hayride, each tale wove together threads of the paranormal and the human experience.

We felt the spectral chill in an old schoolhouse, danced with a phantom at a costume ball, and sat by a bonfire at a haunted campsite. We witnessed a spectral guest disrupting a Halloween feast, saw a scarecrow turn into a vengeful spirit conduit, and listened to the eerie wails of a banshee on All Hallow's Eve.

As we delved deeper into these tales, the shadows grew darker, and the stakes higher. We found restless spirits taking over a peaceful hollow, a family plagued by a Halloween curse, a ghost haunting an old movie theatre, and an otherworldly presence awakened in a library on Halloween night. Our journey led us to the heart of the haunting clock tower, its uncanny thirteenth strike echoing in our ears, and finally to the spectral inhabitants of the Cobweb Castle.

These stories are not mere Halloween tales to be told around a campfire. They are fragments of our shared human experience, slices of the world that we, too often, overlook or dismiss. They serve to remind us that our reality is far more layered and intricate than we might believe. The paranormal is not just the unknown; it is a different lens to view our reality, a way to explore the human condition, our fears, our past, and our connection to the world around us.

In the past two decades of investigating the paranormal, I, Lee Brickley, have come to understand that our fascination with the supernatural stems not just from fear, but from our deep-seated desire to explore the unknown, to push the boundaries of our understanding of reality. Each of these 26 tales stands testament to that, a beacon of human curiosity and bravery against the backdrop of the inexplicable.

I hope, dear reader, that you found in these pages not just chills and thrills, but also a broader perspective on the world around you. May these tales inspire you to look deeper, question more, and, even in the face of the unknown, stand strong. Because, after all, isn't that what Halloween is truly about? Embracing the unknown, celebrating the mysteries of life, and understanding that, sometimes, it's okay to be a little scared.

So, as we part ways, I invite you to carry the spirit of this book, the essence of these tales, not just on Halloween night, but every day. For the world is full of mysteries, and life is but a grand, haunted mansion, waiting to be explored. And who knows? You may yet find your own chilling tale to tell.

Stay curious, stay brave.

Yours in the pursuit of the unknown,

Lee Brickley.

# About the Author

Lee Brickley is an investigator and author with more than 24 titles currently in publication covering a broad range of subjects including true crime, ancient history, the paranormal, and more.

Born in England, Brickley has been a professional writer for more than two decades. He regularly features in the media due to wide interest in his work, and he has made numerous TV appearances.

To read more books by Lee Brickley simply search his name on Amazon.

Printed in Great Britain
by Amazon

30785695R00088